Ecstatic Essays

by

Brent Cheetham

Grosvenor House
Publishing Limited

The right of Brent Cheetham to be identified as the author of this
work has been asserted in accordance with Section 78
of the Copyright, Designs and Patents Act 1988

The book cover picture is copyright to Brent Cheetham

This book is published by
Grosvenor House Publishing Ltd
Link House
140 The Broadway, Tolworth, Surrey, Kt6 7Ht.
www.grosvenorhousepublishing.co.uk

A CIP record for this book
is available from the British Library

ISBN 978-1-78623-847-4

PREFIX

When Francis Bacon first published his series of essays in 1597 they were an unmitigated success. His volumes of short essays on a range of subjects were so popular that an expanded version was printed in 1625 covering a total of 58 topics. This short book is my feeble effort in updating some of the essays of this august British thinker and writer. Some of the subjects he touched on will be dealt with and new subjects will be introduced, as time has rendered not only the subject matter of some of his essays redundant, but also his response to what was then contemporary problems. It is not my objective to merely garnish his views, but to look at them in a more up-to-date light.

We live in a society in which, more often than not, folks are unable to distinguish between a fact and an opinion. One only has to listen to shows like *Any Questions* – to hear a mountain of opinions – but often the ground below is either bare, or littered with selective facts. If so-called political debates meant anything at all, the panellists would listen and change or modify their respective views. However in reality this rarely happens. When is the last time you listened to such a debate, and somebody said, "yep I am sure you are correct, and I am wrong, how much is it to join your party or group and where do I post the cheque?" Political folk are always in a quandary, as they have to decide just who they are speaking to. Not as simple as it seems at first glance. For example any major establishment party will have the media in attendance at their annual conference. But who should they address when speaking, the several thousand delegates laying recumbent in their seats or the several million folks doing the same at home? You can appeal to the non-committed general public or the so-called floating voter, which may go down a bomb. However in doing so you risk alienating your core support, it's impossible to appeal to two disparate groups at the same time and get a favourable result. It's a fine tightrope they walk, which further means any such public speech will be dressed up in a language that appears to say everything, but perhaps if you dig deeper is saying nothing at all. Political language is an enigma to most of us, and indeed Alan Turing of Bletchley Park, would have had a hard job today trying to decipher what our political leaders really mean.

Opinions are not facts – and most, if not all, the Essays in this book are my opinion. Facts can't be challenged, but opinions can. So it's the right, and the duty of any free thinking folk who have had the nerve to attempt to read this diatribe, to question anything and everything that is written within these pages. It's not Gospel, nor some kind of guideline on how to view or deal with the world. I would not be so presumptuous to claim such a thing. Books that assert that they have the answer to the world's political and social problems, I will leave to religious folk and political folk, they are welcome to it. If you the good reader, manage to read this series of missives without falling asleep, or vomiting in a bucket then I have achieved my objective. If it has caused folks to stop and think about things, then that is a big bonus.

THE TRUTH

What is the truth? Not as easy to answer as at first it may seem. We all know the earth goes round the sun, and hopefully we can safely say most folks would deem that to be a truth. However beyond that things become more problematical. Today the most insurmountable problem is that society and many folk are incapable of differentiating a fact from an opinion. Politicians and religious leaders seem strongly addicted and prone to this habit; perhaps there should be some kind of help group like alcoholics anonymous or gamblers anonymous for the poor sufferers of this debilitating illness. I can just image it now at a group therapy meeting, a politician stands up, my name is Joe Bloggs and I just can't help dressing up opinions as facts. They could meet every month and discuss if they have been off the "opinion wagon" over the last month. But knowing politicians they would lie even about that – and have sneaked in the odd opinion when they thought no one was looking. Indeed they would not last long in politics if they started acting in this strange way. Politics is not for the honest, but for the cunning and those who think they are above the rest of us regardless of party.

An honest politician will also remain at the bottom of the heap, and never rise to high office, as honesty is in the realm of others not them. Honesty is deemed as the least desirable attribute as far as establishment political parties are concerned, and I can't see that ever changing. Some folks enter politics as virgins, with a clear heart and mind, but they soon find that they are like a drop of distilled water in a bucket of urine, and will be corrupted with the viscous material around them.

Some folks claim that truth is not a movable object but is static. Yes some truths are – like the Earth going round the sun. Other truths change over time, same as a lie. A lie today could be the truth tomorrow, and a truth today could be a lie tomorrow. Folks often claim that such and such an individual or group are good or bad. However all groups mutate (as do individuals) over time. No sane person would claim for instance that the Labour Party of Keir Hardie would have anything to do with the Labour party of Tony Blair, or that the communism of Joe Stalin had any to do with Mikhail Gorbachev. Likewise religious groups change, often within a short period of time. Jim Jones ran a "Christian revivalist" movement from the mid-1950s until 1978, when his utopia dream was ground to dust on 18 November 1978 when he forced 918 of his adherents to drink cyanide. Thus bringing the largest death toll of American citizens until 9/11. Likewise the Seventh Day Adventist church was seen as a moderate group, who refused to bear arms during World War Two. However the Branch Dravidian's slowly changed under the leadership of its charismatic leader Mr David Koresh, which culminated with a gun battle with American Federal and Texas State law enforcement officers at the siege of Waco in April 1993. As a result of the gun battle and subsequent fire at their compound, 76 folks lost their lives.

So it would not be unfair to say that as religious groups go, they were seen as moderate good folks at the start of the groups, but at the time of their demise, most folk would describe them as extremist, evil folk. But the question is more complex than that, what should folks have called them whilst in transit from good to evil? If folks still called them good halfway through this transition period, would they just be telling a "half truth?" Perhaps some truths are not absolute?

Truth is painless say some of the poets; I think they could not be further from the truth. We all hate to hear the truth about not only ourselves, but about whatever group, we identify with. Seeking anything that approximates to the truth, is not a painless process, as once you are within grasp of that Holy Grail, it morphs into something that is indefinable. Truth to most of us is an ugly beast, like Medusa, as to gaze on it, only turns us to stone. And any person or group, that claims to hold the truth, are not only deluding mankind but also themselves. When folks talk of truth and the answer to world's problem beware. Truth in essence is an answer to a question, so it's best to "question the question". Have they asked the right question in the first place? Take that question mark and turn it on its head, and start again, that is how mankind progresses.

OF REVENGE

They say that revenge is sweet, but what is the point of revenge? Is it to right a wrong, or does it go deeper than that? First of all we have to define what revenge is, as not all revenge is justified. The revenge of a criminal against a police officer who put him/her away for a crime for instance can never be morally justified. And instant revenge is libel to be a Pyrrhic victory, as in publicly assaulting somebody who has done you wrong. Revenge should never go further than to equal things out, as to deal out punishment, which is worse than the damage done to you in the first place is not revenge but an abrogation of moral duty.

Revenge should also be within the law, tempered by reason and not be an eye for an eye, a tooth for a tooth. An extreme case scenario, if someone has murdered your innocent best friend, and you in turn murdered an innocent best friend of the culprit as revenge, you would be no worse than him/her.

Before contemplating revenge, one should ask, has that person really done me harm, and if so did he/she deliberately set out to damage me in any way. We all often get tied down to our own small personal world, where things go out of perspective and it is best to con-template what the man on the Clapham omnibus would think if he was acquainted with all the facts. Most times looking at things in the cold sober light of day, we realize that revenge is meaningless, futile and counterproductive.

Revenge is a human emotion, whether we like it or not and has been with us since the dawn of time. However things done in the spirit of revenge seldom give the revenger a long-term mental calm and easiness, as instant justice without moral thought eats like a canker worm into the soul of the executor of such revenge. In fact it's best not to think of revenge at all, as revenge blinds us to reason. If someone or a group has done you wrong, its best to not think about revenge but think about justice and then act accordingly, within the law. Revenge has not as sweet a taste as some make out, and revenge can lead to a vendetta, which is often hard to break. Always think of the consequences of taking revenge, not only on the person you are taking it out on, but others around you, and last but not least yourself.

ON LOVE

Love can be described as the intense focus of energy towards an individual or object and sometimes including, close friends or relatives of the person your love. It stands to reason that being so intense it's impossible to share the love outside your immediate circle of friends.

When you hear folks say things like, the Queen loves all her subjects, or that Mother Theresa did likewise to all the children in her care worldwide, it sounds silly to say the least. Indeed if you share the love, it diminishes the love given to any one person and the love become less intense. It's almost like saying that a mother who nurses a sick child, does not have the same sense of love that Mother Theresa showed for her orphans. I would put up the argument that a mother who nurses a sick child, has more intense love for that child, as her energy and focus is on that one individual.

And as for the Queen loving her subjects – How do we know that? – has she met all of her subjects to decide for herself? My guess is that, some of her subjects, she would have an intense dislike of if she had the dubious pleasure of meeting them.

When you hear folks, who have just come off holiday saying how great it was, and how they love all the folks, from such and such country – it makes me want to have a reality check. Have they met all the people, from that country? Are not folks paid to be nice to you whilst on holiday? Unless you are unfortunate enough to meet a continental clone of Basil Fawlty whilst abroad – or course they are going to be nice.

Saying you loves all the folks from one country or race, or culture, is a stupid as saying you hate all the folks from one country. As in neither case have you had the acquaintance of an entire country.

Love is often the precursor to hate, as the person or object of your adorations (Which could include football teams etc.) must be defended if offence has been per-ceived to be given against your object of veneration. Extreme love can be just as dangerous as extreme hate. As with most things in life it's better not to be extreme anything!

ON RESPECT

I remember being taught at school, you should always respect your elders and your superiors, otherwise how do expect your inferiors to respect you. Now I am older I can question this ill-advised notion. The very fact that I am old does not mean that younger readers of this essay have to bow to me in a token of respect for writing this.

In essence the above quote, is telling youth that they must not question their elders, as you should always respect folks that are older and wiser then you. Taken at face value, does it mean all old folks are wise? Some folks can go through life like Alexander the Great's donkey, who accompanied him on his military expeditions, but at the end of the day he remained a donkey and learnt nothing from his experience. We should judge older folks (and give them respect, when due) not on the fact they are old alone, but on their intellectual prowess. The youth should not take the word and wisdom, of the old, as being gospel truth, but make rational judgments as to the validity of their statements.

The second issue with this statement is who decides who are our superiors and who are our inferiors. It appears to me that in today's climate superiority is decided by one thing only – wealth. But does wealth automatically make you a clever chap or lady – I think not? Sometimes you can get more common sense from a humble welsh sheep farmer than our so-called superiors.

To hell with this talk of superiors and inferiors, as unless you are an imbecile, we can all excel at things, that others can't (or will not) do. As with all things in life, treat everybody the same, be they a lord or lady, or a dustman or a shop girl. Be they rich or poor, black or white, religious or non-religious or even supporters of the Cliff Richard fan club. This will not always bring happy results, as some folks will take umbrage, for not showing them due subservient obsequiousness. If this happens, then it's them who have who have abrogated their rights to be a decent member of the human race and not you. Let them have sleepless nights about your lack of respect and not you.

CULTS

When one thinks of cults, one tends to think of religious cults. However history has shown that there have been cults that have no basis in religion whatsoever. Think of the cults around Hitler, Stalin and Chairman Mao. It's been said it is hard to define what a cult is, and I suppose at one time when Christianity was first born, it could be called a cult. Does a religion become a non-cult when it becomes mainstream?

For the purposes of this short essay, I will take the liberty of defining a cult, as worship, of an individual, group or religion, which insists you don't ask questions. All cults tell their members to suspend their powers of critical observation, and to view any folks outside their world-view as being unworthy and not deserving of respect.

I have heard folks say – why criticize folks in a religious cult, if such a cult gives them comfort and joy? My reply would be have they seen the films taken in Germany in the 1930s of crowds cheering their leader Mr Adolf Hitler. They sure have comfort and joy worshiping their leader. Therefor it would be wrong to question the Nazis? Crystal meth, gives folks comfort and joy, whilst they use it, would it be wrong to question those who supply and partake in its use? At the end of the day, no individual leader, no political group (be they left or right), no religion (be they a cult or not), should be beyond reproach. The world needs more liberty, and questioning today, then it ever has, so don't allow folks to close down debate in the name of any cause.

MORALS

How many times have we heard folks go on about morals? The country has gone to the dogs and has lost its morals is a not uncommon one. But what are morals, I think most of us can agree, that it's wrong, to mug an old lady, or anybody else for that matter. We can agree that it's wrong to murder folk and torture folk, or to bear false witness. However when folks talk about morals, they are often are referring to sexual morals. No sex before marriage; going to church on a Sunday morning; eating over the period of lent; reading the wrong type of licentious book or viewing an immoral film. Persons who say these things are in effect claiming they are morally perfect and better than the rest of mankind, who they view as being morally defective in some way.

Morals to my small mind are often locked into a cultural/religious box that takes time to change for the better. At one time it was thought moral, to hang witches, burn heretics, or torture folk during the Spanish inquisition. Folks, who did these things, believed at the time that what they were doing was moral. Likewise the Nazi's shooting; gassing or incarcerating Jews and others in concentration camps to be used as slave labour fell within the Nazi view of high moral conduct. The same can be said for Stalin and his Gulags.

High morals should rise above cultural restraints, and be viewed with one simple question. Do my morals impose on others or are they harmful to any third party. If they do, then it's time to ditch those morals?

PERSONAL PREFERENCES

We all have personal preferences, be they the type of music we like, the books we read, the religion we choose (or none), the political party or sporting team we support etc... The human race is diverse, and it would be a boring and dull place if we all liked identical things. A prosaic example that this diverse world can bring is the world of music. Sometimes you hear more mature folk saying, this modern rock and roll music is crap, and likewise you sometimes hear, some members of the younger generation proclaim that classical music or opera music is crap.

No music is crap; it all depends on the ear of the listener. And although it maybe crap to you others may enjoy their audio pleasure. So in a free country feel free to enjoy whatever stimulates your eardrums, be it Gregorian chant, opera, classical music, rock and roll or even Cliff Richard. Let's not waste our time denigrating other folks form of enjoyment; it just makes for unnecessary conflict!

WEALTH CREATORS

Wealth creators are two words bandied about by our political elites, to define financers and entrepreneurs who supposedly make the world go round all by themselves. But do they really create wealth as our political master's claim? I could be wealthy and own vast tracts of land, or own factories, warehouses or shopping centres. However before I could make a penny there is one missing ingredient from the equation – that is human beings. No business can operate without personnel, right down to the cleaners in a factory, manual workers, and tractor drivers on a farm, office staff, and a myriad of other staff. In short, no matter how rich folks are they need others to make the world go around. It can be said that the most important people in a hospital, are not the surgeons, doctors or administration staff (although sometimes they think they have the most important job in the world and are often paid appropriately). By far the most important people are the hospital cleaners, it's no good having the best surgeon in the world operate on you, only to pick up some virus or bug such as MRSA or E Coli due to ineffective cleaning. To be wealth creators the system must work at all levels (hospitals nowadays are run as economic concerns).

In the natural world, many disparate life forms have a symbiotic relationship with each other. The same is true with business. The bosses could not survive without the workers (and everybody in between). And the workers could not survive without the bosses. If the workers were bees, and flowers were bosses, it's clear that flowers could not survive without the bees and other insects and the bees could not survive without the flowers. It's about time that the bosses and the workers acknowledge this symbiotic relationship and did not treat the others as if they were some alien species. Woking together as a team in business may be a pipe dream that may never come to fruition – that's life. But a harmonious relationship within business is something that is worth striving for, as it can reap large benefits for both sides. But before this can even be attempted both sides have to admit that a symbiotic relationship does exists, and that no one is superior to the other – that would be a good place to start!

ON ATHEISM

A recent YouGov poll claimed that 62% of folks in the UK claim to be "non-religious". For most people atheism would appear to mean that they just don't attend church any more. They are non-active folk who for whatever reason have rejected religion as part of their daily life. Sometimes when you listen to religious extremists you would think they are all amoral folk, living the life of a rake or harlot. The simple fact appears that most are no more amoral than religious folk, who by design or implication are of a secular disposition – as are many religious folk. The only time you will see them in church is for "Hatchings, Matchings and Dispatchings" (Births, marriages and funerals). And then only out of a matter of respect for others and they often feel they have a moral obligation to attend.

My contention is that most atheist are not any kind of threat to religious folk, however there is a small vocal minority, who have gone beyond the thinking of the likes of Richard Dawkins, who think that all religions should be banned and their places of worship torn down and I write this essay in response to this, giving three main objections.

1. If we believe in a free country and the free rights of men (or women), then we should support the right to worship either collectively or individually who or whatever folks want. This right to worship does not extend to imposing your will on others, be they other religions or non-believers. Nor should your group be granted special privileges over other religious groups. All religions must abide by the law of the land. They should have the right to give a critique of other religions, politicians, and non-religious folk, provided it does not extend into any form of encouragement to hatred. They must also accept that the right to give a critique should extend to others who may wish to question their views. The right to criticize must at all times be reciprocal. The religion must also do no harm to others including adherents of the faith (Otherwise you could have some group sacrificing a young virgin to appease some god). If all the above are adhered to, I can't see any need for curtailing or banning any religion. So my first objections are on moral grounds.

2. The second reason is purely pragmatic. Just how would this work? The chances of burning or destroying every religious book in the world must be somewhat nebulous. If folks still think this is the way forward they should be challenged. And even if they did succeed, no doubt somebody or folks will find a new god to worship. To use the vernacular of today, "It's a no brainer".

3. To destroy old religious monuments and places of worship over the centuries has usually been the

work of religious rivals. (Why is it that religious extremists feel the need to don the mantle of pyromaniacs and burn down other folks places of worship)? For atheist or others to do the same casts them in the same mould, as the religious extremists who they find abhorrent. Two peas from the same pod? Last but not least old religious buildings are part of our inheritance and many folks including me find them atheistically pleasing.

SOME RELIGIOUS CONUNDRUMS

God gave his only son for the forgiveness of sin – is often quoted in religious circles. However it's not clear to me if they are talking about past sins, present sins, or sins committed in the future. If it's past sins, does it mean that god has gone down to hell, opened the gates, and let them into heaven? If that is the case there is no such thing as hell, or if there is it's empty? And if it is future sins, does that mean folks can sin and they will still be going to heaven?

The second problem I have with this is that nobody can grant forgiveness on behalf of a third party. If somebody does me harm I can forgive them, but I can't forgive them on behalf of somebody else that person has done harm to, it's a physical impossibility?

Thirdly, the statement that god gave his only son, is contrary to what the Bible preaches, as according to the good book, Jesus ascended into heaven to be with god, and Christians are awaiting his second coming. It's like lending your neighbour your lawn mower after his lawn mower has broken down, and taking it back the next day. After all you would not say in this instance, that you gave your lawn mower to your neighbour.

And last but not least, if Jesus was God's son, and we are all mammals so therefore god must have had a wife, but there is not mention of a Mrs God in the Bible. The only alternative is that God made Jesus, as he made us, in his image. But if God made us, then who made God? Perhaps God has his own God and an altar at which to worship him, and does that God have his own God and an altar, which to worship him on, and so on ad-infinitum?

IDENTITY POLITICS

Some years ago I recall Mr Nick Griffin, leader of the British National Party, made a comment about him or his party speaking on behalf on the British people. Many folks at the time, quite rightly in my view, questioned this saying he or his party do not speak on behalf of the British people, but only on behalf of a relatively small number of followers.

No one can speak on behalf of any group, be it a political group, a country, a religious group or whatever. When it comes down to religion, too many folks have accepted the template offered up by some religious leaders, as you often hear comments about the Christian community, the Jewish community, the Muslim community etc, etc. But with any such so-called group, there is diversity of thought not only within the leadership, but between individual adherents. To class all Christians as being the same is intellectual laziness. Not only do you have a myriad of different denominations, but different beliefs within them. Christians include anything from nudism, acceptance of homosexuality, to non-acceptance of homosexuality, Snake worship (todays Christian snake handlers, claim they don't worship the snake, but handle the snakes to prove that God will protect them) to Christian Armenian Goat Sacrifice. Likewise with Jews you have Zionist Jews non Zionist Jews, Extremist Zionist Jews to moderate Zionist Jews. You also have anti-Zionist Jews like the Neturei Karta. Muslims are the same, from extremist Muslims right the way through to moderate, liberal Muslims. So to my mind to speak negatively (or positively) about any group as if they were one homogenous group is crass stupidity. And yet many folks and sections of the mass media still talk in these tones.

This leads us on to identity politics. There is a natural human weakness for folks to want to be a member of a group. This can allow for folks that today we describe as having learning difficulties to feel they are part off (and get protection from) a larger group. Taken to extreme, this has and probably will always cause problems for mankind. It seems to me that too many folks learn to identify only with their group, which could be a political group, a race group, religious group or even something like a football team. The problem with identity politics is that folks will always back up their respective group (my country, right or wrong comes to mind) no matter the circumstances. We get blind to our own faults and failings whist we exaggerate the faults and failings of others. In short we are liable to become narrow-minded and bigoted. Yes by all means feel free to belong or join any group, but please bear in mind that others are not members of your group and treat them the same as you would want them to treat you. And if you hold moderate liberal values, you should not change from that just because another group or person does not espouse them.

THE MIDDLE CLASS

Although most of us hate to admit it, we tend to think of ourselves as the centre of the universe and no doubt nature has given us a good reason for doing so, as a survival strategy. It's as if the world would collapse if we were not in control or running things. Books of condolences are full of the names of folk, who thought the world would stop spinning without them. Part of nature's survival for the individual is to attach oneself to a larger group, be it a nation or a state, or a group within that state. One such group can be loosely called the middle class. In the days of Karl Marx, this was clearly defined by economic income. Not so much nowadays as it's more defined by an attitude of mind, which subverts any freethinking into a form of group thinking. Status is everything. Although one must be above a certain income to join the class. Clearly unemployed folk would not be considered middle class (unless it was a short-term unemployment between jobs), nor would manual labourers, although such folk could earn as much as them.

If there is such a thing as a dead class it's the middle class, as both the upper class and the working class tend to say what they feel and have no reason to want to impress others. This dead class often has the inability to laugh at themselves as they talk in an echo chamber of their own insecurity. Laughing out loud, is for the working class and the upper class, but not for the middle class, as its seen as crass and stupid and not the "done thing". They always appear to be looking over their shoulders, making sure they have said the right thing, and have not upset anybody in the unofficial pecking order. When talking with them they appear to be false and phony, as they talk in a form of code, which is not too hard to decipher. They may mock other groups that talk their own version of the English language, forgetting that they do the same. You will hear phrase like; I don't approve of that, i.e. I don't approve of gay marriage, I don't approve of my daughter going out with somebody from a council estate and so on. When they use the phrase I don't approve – all it means is "it's not the law, but if I had my way it would be the law" – and when some of them go on about gay marriage, it's to show how superior and virtuous they are over folks who may be inclined towards that sexual proclivity. It's an interesting thing to note, that although such things as this are often said in company, I feel sure many middle class folk deep in their hearts don't believe what is being propounded in those circles. The simple fact that what their group think forces them to say nothing, and act like nodding donkeys, rather than question things, as questioning things means you will be ostracised from the group – and that would never do – status and the pecking order is everything.

Although I offer up this humble critique of the middle class, I cannot see anybody or any group finding a solution to the problem. Finding the solution to this problem as likely as finding the Holy Grail, being somewhat nebulous, as perhaps there is none (as any solution would be short lived – until a new middle class comes into being). I only hope that any middle class folk who have had the unmitigated audacity to read this short essay are not too offended by its contents.

ON THE FEAR OF FAILURE

One of the biggest excuses for not doing something is the subconscious fear of failure. We all fear failure, as failure is often subject to public ridicule. If you can't countenance failure your life on earth will be wasted, as you will never achieve anything and just be an also ran following in the footsteps of others. Real men and woman are made or sterner stuff, as the folks who have made changes in the world have always comes up against opposition. Here are some brief details of such folk, who fought against the odds, with the prospect of failure always on the horizon.

Emmeline Pankhurst 1858–1928, the great speaker for the women's suffragette movement. It's often forgotten today, that it was not just men who opposed her as she had to fight woman like the redoubtable Mrs Humphry Ward 1851–1920 an English novelist who ran the "Woman's National anti-suffrage league". Whilst Mrs Pankhurst and her followers, were marching for universal suffrage, Mrs Ward and her followers (she was supported by the liberal MP Hilaire Belloc) marched in the opposite direction shouting "No votes for women". Thank God Emmeline Pankhurst did not fear failure.

The slavery abolitionists Thomas Clarkson 1760–1846 and William Wilberforce 1759–1833, had years of failure before they got the slave trade abolished. Failure did not deter them!

If you set out to achieve something, or change the way we think, you could end up paying a high price for your endeavours. You will always upset the establishment, as you have no choice but to ruffle a few feathers, in the course of which you will become intensely disliked.

The Dutch Jewish philosopher Baruch Spinoza 1632–77 was subjected to "Hegal" by the Jewish religious authorities for his biblical criticism (Hegal is the Jewish equivalent to being excommunicated by the catholic church) and for his efforts was placed on the Catholic church's index for forbidden books. Today he is seen as one of the world's greatest philosophers. He did not let the thought of failure get in his way.

Galileo Galilei the famous astronomer and mathematician 1564–1642 was jailed for life for "Heresy that contradicts Holy Scripture". And yet few folks today would call him a failure.

The Franciscan Monk and philosopher William Ockham, 1632–77, famous for his "Occam's razor" ended up by being excommunicated by the church for his efforts. But failure appears to have never been a word in his dictionary.

So spurn failure as you would a poisonous snake, and banish the world failure from your vocabulary.

SOME MAXIMS AND DEFINITIONS

A politician – A person who tells you what the best thing for you is, but only thinking about the best thing for him or her self.

Parish Councillors – Parliament in microcosm – Folks who think they are important and clever, and look upon themselves as miniature versions, of Winston Churchill, or Margaret Thatcher.

Blasphemy – A devise made up by the church in old times, to protect the power of the church, as the god who made the universe is not strong enough to not get upset by a few profaners.

Tired and emotional – An expression used by solicitors to excuse the behaviour of their drunken client.

New and improved recipe – A product that is on sale, but using cheaper ingredients.

To be honest with you – A phrase used to sales staff, when they are lying to you.

Devout – Never trust a person who says they are a devout anything, as they are too blinkered, and are unable to see things outside their enclosed bubble.

District and county councillors – Folks who are just jumped up parish councillors but with more clout.

Cliff Richards fans – Folks who are convinced he will save the world.

Pop idols – Folks who think the world is there to serve and save them.

Robust – A word used by the police force after there is a problem – to describe the fact that they will do nothing – as in a "Robust response".

We have to look at all the alternatives – A sentence used by politicians to say why they are doing nothing, and they don't propose to take any actions on the matter either.

Insanity is rare in an individual – but in groups it is not a phenomenon, but ubiquitous!

Fashion – Folks, who follow fashion, are folks who are too weak to forge their own identity.

Extreme right wingers – Folks who think they are 100% right and others are 100% wrong.

Extreme left wingers – folks who say the others are 100% wrong and they are 100% right.

Green folks – Folks who want to save the planet, but can't save their local green belt from being built on.

ON BOOKS

As human beings we like to think of ourselves as being in control. We view the world around us, and the people within it, and wish we could mould both the world and the people in it to our image and to our way of thinking. As we are all unique individuals any attempts to radically change the way folks act is fraught with problems, and is bound to end in tears. We can alter the way folks think and act, but we can't change folks completely, as that is the way nature designed us. Folks, who have tried this in the past, have ended up being bloody dictators.

The natural world around us seems an abomination, all chaos, and beyond our control. Perhaps this desire for control has found outlets with some humans, as they take up gardening in a manifest attempt to control something that is beyond control. Nature did not intend plants, and trees to grow in regimented rows, nor to have round or square flowerbeds. Nature still dictates the terms, as we have to plant the flowers and do the pruning when nature decides and not us. Maybe that's why some gardeners say they feel they are closer to nature whilst they are gardening. But they are wrong, they are not closer to nature, they are just one part of nature.

Not only are we all unique, but we all see and hear things differently. It depends on our mindset how we view the world. Some folks will say they love a piece of music or a painting, whilst others can take a negative view to the same piece of music or painting. We can sometimes be indifferent, to a piece of music or a painting and yet years later we can hear the same music or view the same picture and something clicks inside our heads and we either love it or hate it. It depends what frame of mind folks have in their approach to the subject matter.

Books are the food of mankind, as without them we are starved of human knowledge. Whilst films and plays have their place in society they are limited in what they can offer. Any film is but a visual and sound interpretation of a book, or a scriptwriter. The work of interpretation is done for you, and you have no need to use your imagination. It's a lazy person's form of entertainment. Books can describe sights and sounds – and when a book talks of sounds like church bells ringing, or the sound of a train hooting, or a fog horn, the brain reproduces those sounds inside our head from memory – but everybody hears them slightly different from others, as all our memories are not the same.

If a book describes a scene or a person – each of us visualises that scene or person in a different way – no matter how detailed the writer has been. So in a perverse way, each book we see on a shelf is a unique book, and a one off first edition. As the same book can be read by many different people, but they all have different interpretations of the book, and take in different amounts of information.

If folks have read a book years ago it can be an interesting exercise to re-read the book. You can often find, it's like reading a new book, you think to yourself how did I miss that, or that's not how I remember that scene. Our minds and our brains can play tricks with us. We think we are in control of our minds, but we are not, our minds control us.

ON PEACE AND
TRANQUILLITY.

We all need time out from the hustle and bustle of everyday life, be it your work place or if you are parents trying to balance work, parenting and play. Peace and tranquillity does not mean your brain should cease to function, rather the opposite. Peace gives you that all-important commodity, which is lacking in today's society – time.

Time to get your thoughts together, time to contemplate beautiful scenery, and think to yourself that the view in front of you will never be the same again, clouds change, colours change and no one else will ever have the experience that you are indulging in right now.

Whilst at work many folks have to make decisions in haste and on the hop, which can turn out to have a deleterious effect on your work place. Now is the time to measure and weight things up and think free thoughts, without the input of others. Now is the time to dream and work out how your future dreams can come to fruition.

Now is the time to stop thinking, and put this book down, as your sleepy eyes get the better of you (I am told that most folk read just before going to bed). So to you my good and patient reader, good night, sleep tight, and sorry for the theft of your valuable time.

Lightning Source UK Ltd.
Milton Keynes UK
UKHW010623080222
398373UK00001B/162